Sight Word Stories

Learn to Read 120 Words within Meaningful Content

"I Can Read Story 5"
can – me – too

Me Too!

**by
Sherrill B. Flora**

"I Can Read Story 7"
play – with – you – yes

Can I Play With You?

"I Can Read Story 9"
what – do – want

What Do You Want To Do?

**illustrated by
Vanessa Countryman**

"I Can Read Story 8"
Review Story

Little Dog and Big Cat Play

"I Can Read Story 19"
he – ran – away

He Ran Away!

**Publisher
Key Education Publishing Company, LLC
Minneapolis, Minnesota**

Credits
Author: Sherrill B. Flora
Inside Illustrations: Vanessa Countryman
Creative Director: Mary Claire
Cover Design: Mary Eden
Editor: George C. Flora

Key Education welcomes manuscripts and product ideas from teachers.
For a copy of our submission guidelines, please send a self-addressed, stamped envelope to:

Key Education Publishing Company, LLC
Acquisitions Department
9601 Newton Avenue South
Minneapolis, Minnesota 55431

ISBN: 1-933052-10-4
Sight Word Stories
Copright © 2005 Key Education Publishing Company, LLC
Minneapolis, Minnesota 55431

Introduction

What are sight words and why are they so important? Sight words are considered to be those words that people should be able to look at and instantly identify. Many sight words are not spelled phonically, so consequently it is not possible to "sound them out." People simply need to recognize them by "sight." A majority of sight words are also considered to be high-frequency words—those words that make up nearly fifty-percent of the words that we use and read.

Sight Word Stories is a delightful book that contains twenty-five, eight-page reproducible, humorous, and predictable storybooks. These stories will introduce children to over seventy high-frequency sight words and an additional forty easy-to-phonically-read words. The words presented in *Sight Word Stories* have been researched and compiled from the following well respected high-frequency and grade level word lists:

- Dolch Basic Sight Vocabulary
- American Heritage Word Frequency Book
- Starter Words
- A Basic Vocabulary of Elementary School Children

Mastery of these important words will motivate young readers, boost their reading test scores, and increase their fluency and comprehension. Help the students you teach to become successful readers by having them master the essential sight word vocabulary contained in *Sight Word Stories!*

Contents

Introduction 3
Word Lists 4

Story 1 – big, little, and
Big Cat and Little Dog..................................... 5–6
Story 2 – up, am, down
Up and Down 7–8
Story 3 – come, here, good
Come Here! 9–10
Story 4 – like, to, run, I
I Like To Run! 11–12
Story 5 – can, me, too
Me Too! 13–14
Story 6 – look, at, the
The Forest 15–16
Story 7 – play, with, you, yes
Can I Play With You?......................................17–18
Story 8 – Review Story
Little Dog and Big Cat Play 19–20
Story 9 – what, do, want
What Do You Want To Do? 21–22
Story 10 – funny, that, see, sees
Funny Pets 23–24
Story 11 – we, will, ride, on
Let's Ride! 25–26
Story 12 – one, two, three
One, Two, Three! 27–28
Story 13 – is, in, find
Look and Find 29–30

Story 14 – go, get, help
Get Help! 31–32
Story 15 – where, are, my
Where Are My Pets?.. 33–34
Story 16 – Review Story
Help Little Dog and Big Cat 35–36
Story 17 – said, did, it, jump
See It Jump! 37–38
Story 18 – who, was, she
Who Was She? 39–40
Story 19 – he, ran, away
He Ran Away! 41–42
Story 20 – this, for, happy
Happy Birthday! 43–44
Story 21 – have, a, new
New Toys! 45–46
Story 22 – no, now, not, out
Come Out and Play..47–48
Story 23 – make, made, pretty
What Did You Make? 49–50
Story 24 – they, all
Who Can? 51–52
Story 25 – Review Story
What Did You Do?...53–54

Sight Word Flash Cards 55–60
Additional Word Flash Cards 61–64

Alphabetical Sight Word List	Sight Word List in Sequential Order	Additional Words

Alphabetical Sight Word List		Sight Word List in Sequential Order			Additional Words
a	pretty	**Story 1:**	**Story 10:**	**Story 18:**	barn
all	ride	big	funny	who	bear/bears
am	ran	little	that	was	beds
and	run	and	see	she	bike
are	said		sees		bird
at	see	**Story 2:**		**Story 19:**	birthday
away	sees	up	**Story 11:**	he	boy
big	she	am	we	ran	box
can	that	down	will	away	bug
come	the		ride		button
did	they	**Story 3:**	on	**Story 20:**	cat
do	three	come		this	dog
down	this	here	**Story 12:**	for	dolls
find	to	good	one	happy	deer
for	too		two		eat
funny	two	**Story 4:**	three	**Story 21:**	elephant
get	up	like		have	fish
go	want	to	**Story 13:**	a	forest
good	was	run	is	new	fox
happy	we	I	in		friends
have	what		find	**Story 22:**	frog
he	where	**Story 5:**		no	giraffe
help	who	can	**Story 14:**	now	girls
here	will	me	go	not	hop
I	with	too	get	out	house
in	yes		help		kitten
is	you	**Story 6:**		**Story 23:**	merry-go-round
it		look	**Story 15:**	make	mess
jump		at	where	made	mouse
like		the	are	pretty	owl
little			my		painting
look		**Story 7:**		**Story 24:**	pets
made		play	**Story 16:**	they	planes
make		with	Review	all	playdough
me		you	Story		puppy
my		yes		**Story 25:**	racoon
new			**Story 17:**	Review	roller coaster
no		**Story 8:**	said	Story	shirt
not		Review	did		shoe
now		Story	it		sock
on			jump		squirrel
one		**Story 9:**			swings
out		what			toy/toys
play		do			trains
		want			tree
					zip

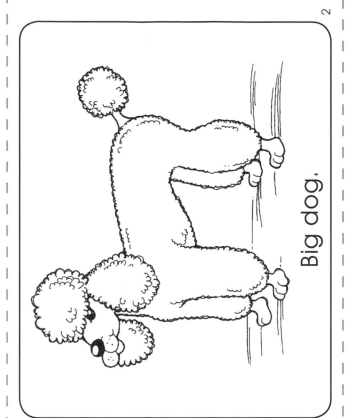

Big dog.

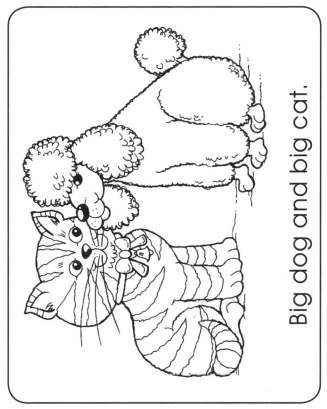

Big dog and big cat.

"I Can Read Story 1"
big – little – and

Big Cat
and
Little Dog

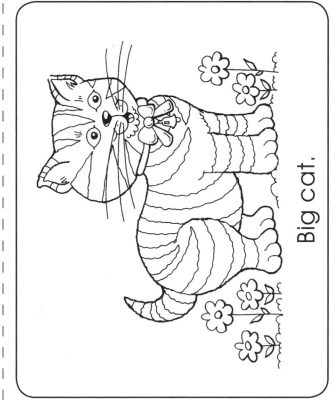

Big cat.

Sight Word Stories

6

Little cat.

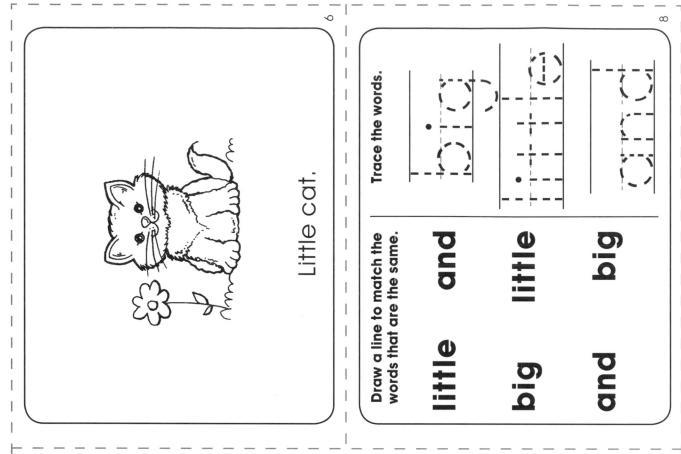

5

Little dog.

7

Little dog and big cat.

8

Trace the words.

Draw a line to match the words that are the same.

little   and

big   little

little   big

and   big

"I Can Read Story 2"

up – am – down

Up and Down

I am up.

I am up.

I am down.

I am down.

6

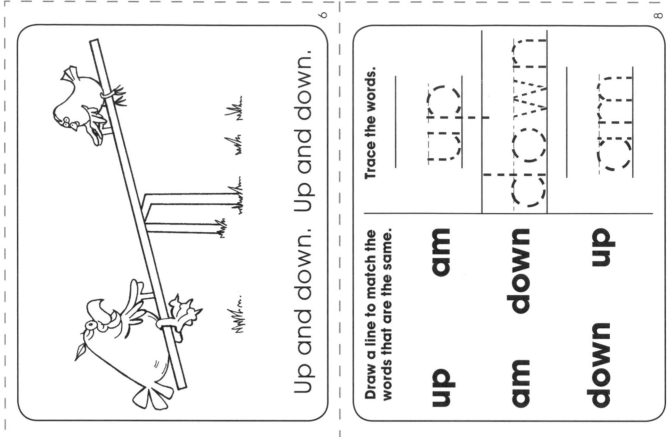

Up and down. Up and down.

8

Trace the words.

Draw a line to match the words that are the same.

up   am

am   down

down

5

I am down.

7

Down! Down! Down!

Come here little bird.

Come here little bug.

"I Can Read Story 3"

come – here – good

Come Here!

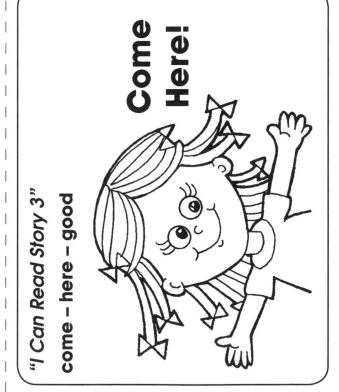

Good little bird.

6

Come here little frog.

8

Trace the words.

come

here

good

Draw a line to match the words that are the same.

come   here

here   good

good   come

5

Good little bug.

7

Good little bird.
Good little bug.
Good little frog.

2

I like to run.

4

I like to run up.

"I Can Read Story 4"

like – to – run – I

I Like To Run!

M

1

3

I like to run and run.

6

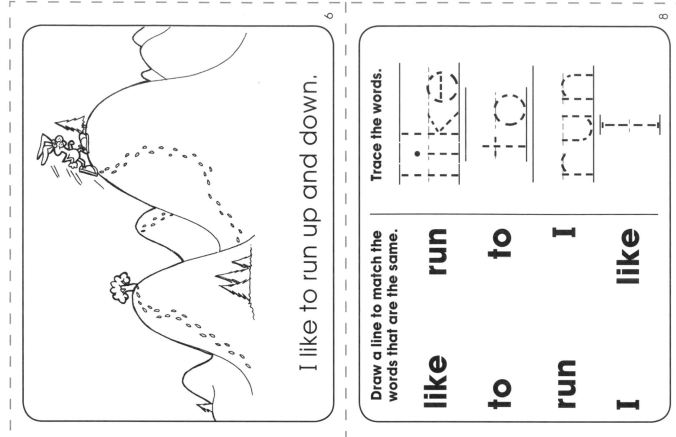

I like to run up and down.

8

Trace the words.

Draw a line to match the words that are the same.

run   like

to   to

I   run

like   I

5

I like to run down.

7

Run! Run! Run!

2

I can run.

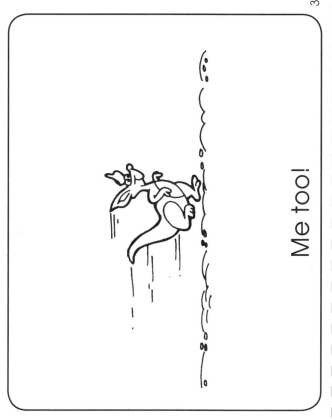

4

I can hop!

"I Can Read Story 5"
can – me – too

Me
Too!

1

3

Me too!

6

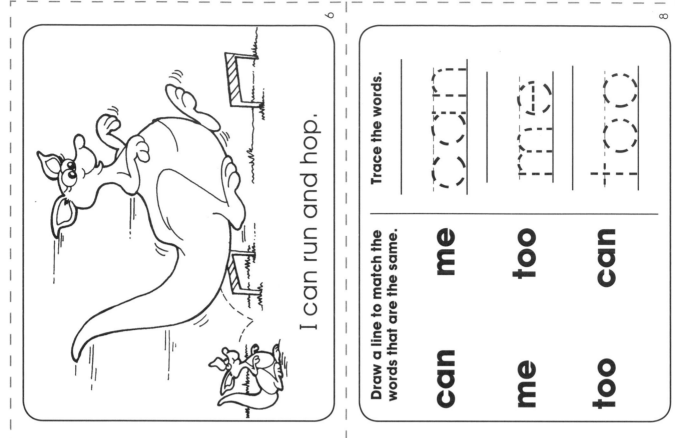

I can run and hop.

8

Trace the words.

Draw a line to match the words that are the same.

can	me
me	too
too	can

5

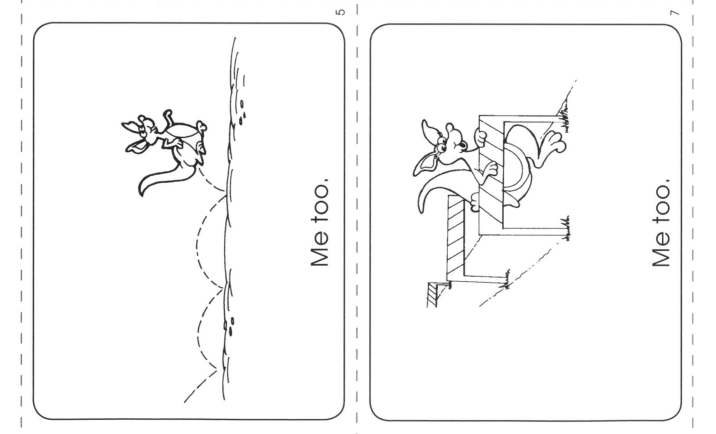

Me too.

7

Me too.

14

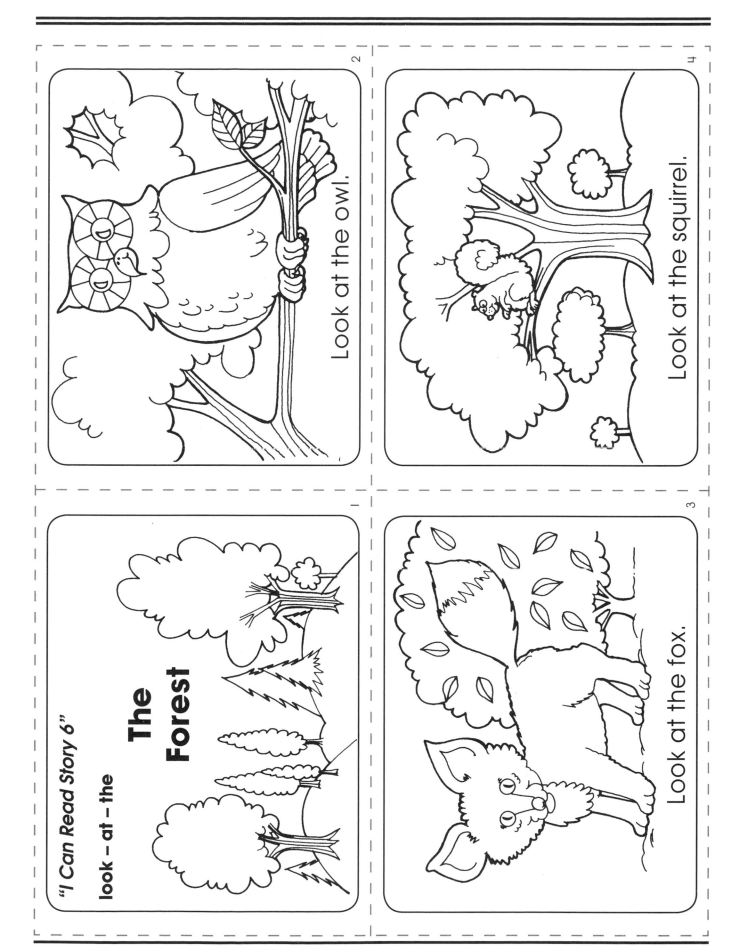

2

Look at the owl.

4

Look at the squirrel.

1

"I Can Read Story 6"

look – at – the

The Forest

3

Look at the fox.

6

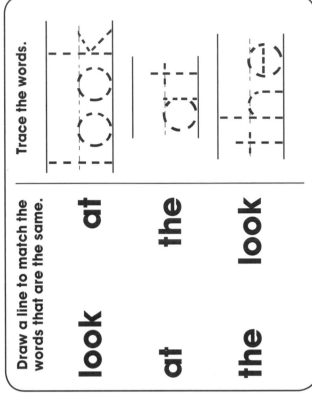

Look at the racoon.

8

Trace the words.

Draw a line to match the words that are the same.

look   at

at   the

the   look

5

Look at the deer.

7

Look at the forest friends.

2

Bear, can I play with you?

4

Bears, can I play with you?

1

"I Can Read Story 7"
play – with – you – yes

Can I Play With You?

3

Yes! Yes!

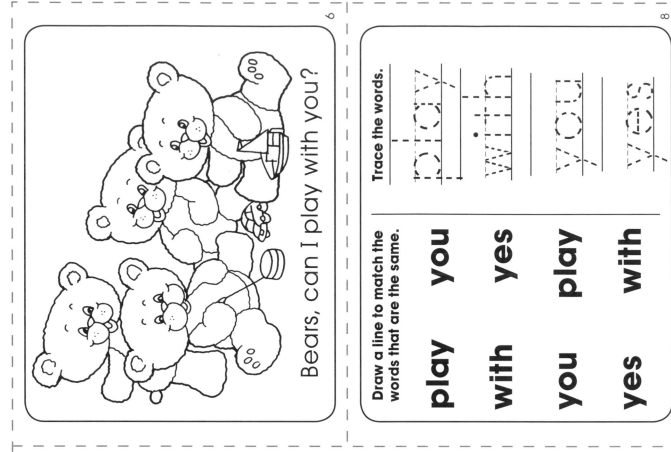

6

Bears, can I play with you?

8

Trace the words.

play with you yes

Draw a line to match the words that are the same.

play   you

with   yes

you   play

yes   with

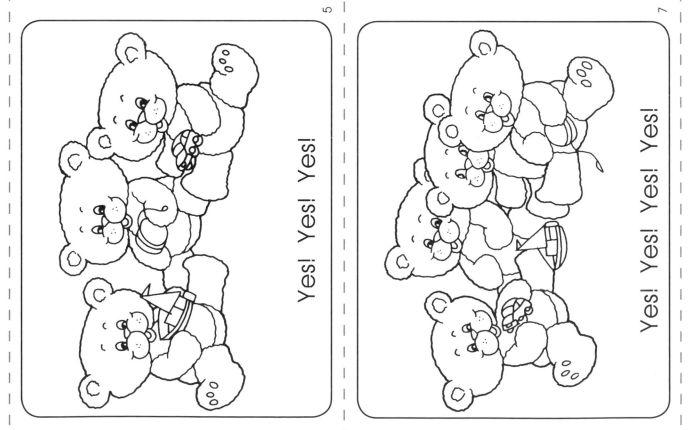

5

Yes! Yes! Yes!

7

Yes! Yes! Yes! Yes!

The little dog and
the big cat like to run.

Come here big cat.
Come here little dog.

"I Can Read Story 8"
Review Story

Little Dog and
Big Cat Play

The big cat and the
little dog run up and down.

6

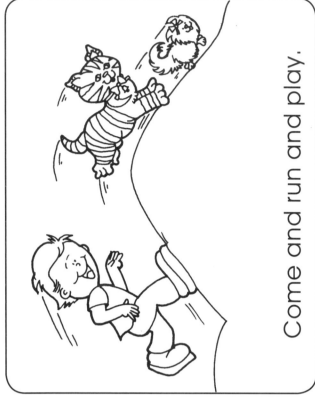

Come and run and play.

8

Finish each sentence with words from the story.

1. _____ dog and _____ cat.

2. Come _____ run _____ play.

3. I can _____ with you.

4. Come here big _____.

5. Come here little _____.

6. I like to _____ and _____.

5

I can run with you.

7

I like to run and play with
little dog and big cat.

2

Monkey,
what do you want to do?

4

Elephant,
what do you want to do?

1

"I Can Read Story 9"
what – do – want

What Do You Want To Do?

3

I want to eat.

6

Giraffe,
what do you want to do?

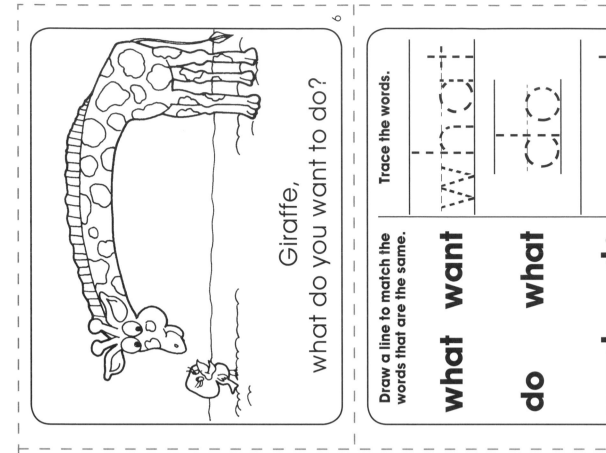

8

Trace the words.

Draw a line to match the words that are the same.

what   what

do

want   do

5

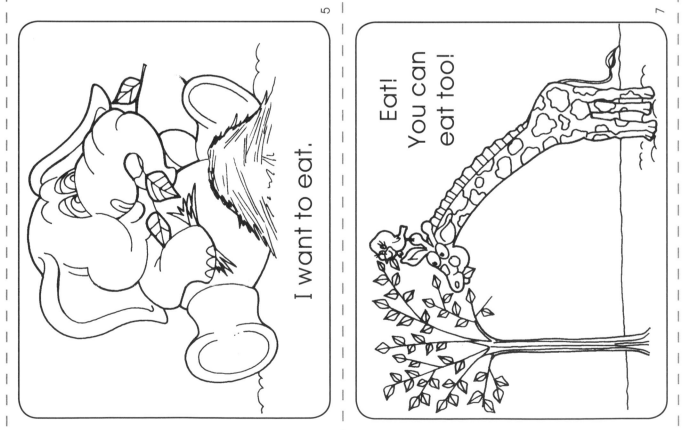

I want to eat.

7

Eat!
You can
eat too!

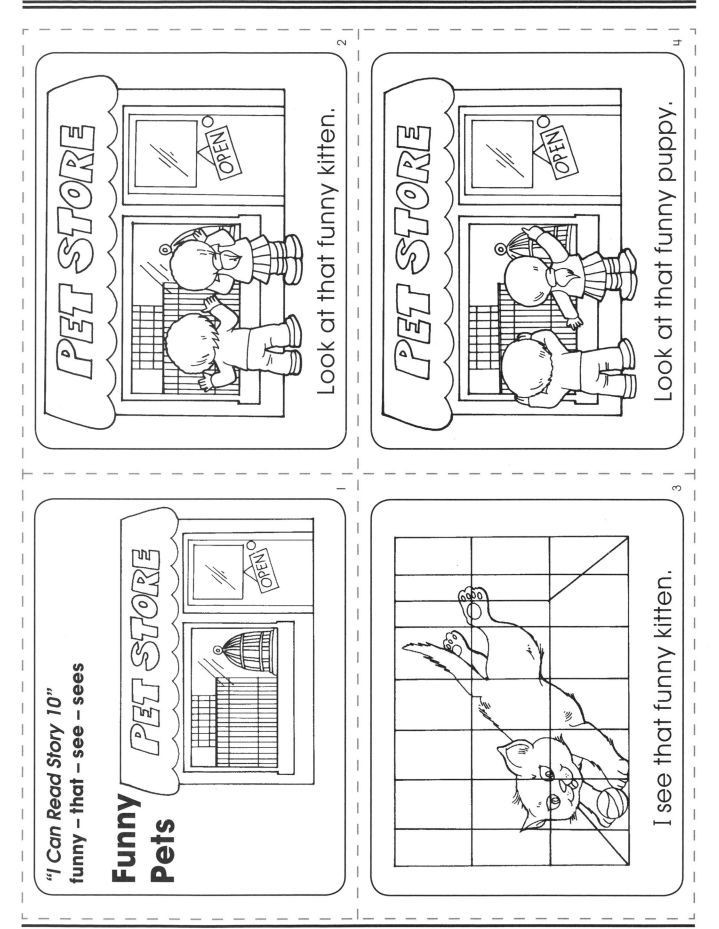

"I Can Read Story 10"
funny – that – see – sees

**Funny
Pets**

PET STORE

1

PET STORE

Look at that funny kitten.

2

I see that funny kitten.

3

PET STORE

Look at that funny puppy.

4

6

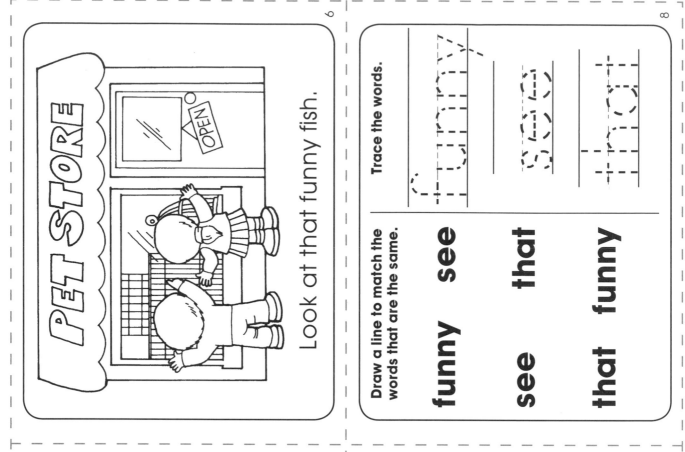

Look at that funny fish.

8

Trace the words.

Draw a line to match the words that are the same.

funny   see

see   that

that   funny

5

I see that funny puppy.

7

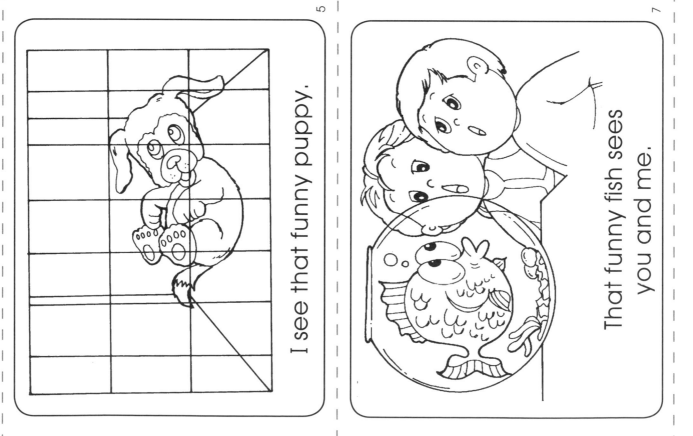

That funny fish sees you and me.

2

We will ride on the planes.

4

We will ride on the swings.

"*I Can Read Story 11*"
we – will – ride – on

Let's Ride!

1

3

We will ride on the trains.

6

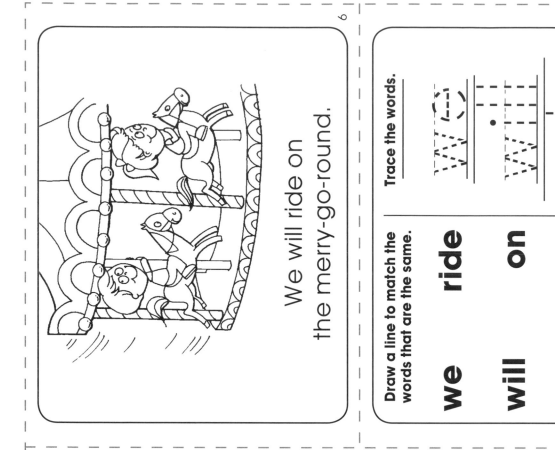

We will ride on
the merry-go-round.

8

Trace the words.

**Draw a line to match the
words that are the same.**

we	**ride**
will	**on**
ride	**will**
on	**we**

5

We will ride
on the roller coaster.

7

Ride and ride and ride!

"*I Can Read Story 12*"
one – two – three

One, Two, Three!

One little bike . . . .

and one little boy.

Two little dolls . . . .

6

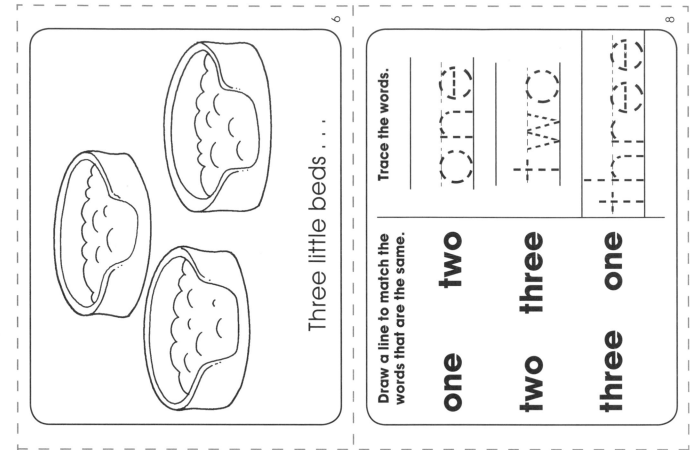

Three little beds . . .

8

Trace the words.

one

two

three

Draw a line to match the words that are the same.

one   two

two   three

three   one

5

and two little girls.

7

and three little kittens.

Sight Word Stories

Find the sock.

Find the shoe.

"I Can Read Story 13"
is – in – find

Look and Find

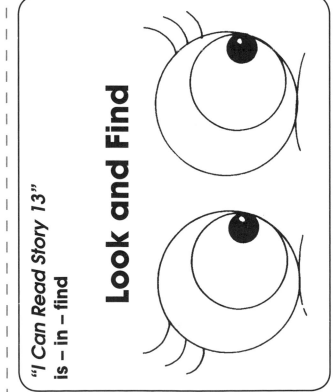

The sock is in the box.

6

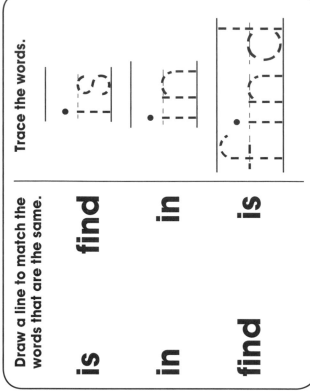

Find the shirt.

8

Trace the words.

is

in

find

Draw a line to match the words that are the same.

is   find

in   in

is   find

5

The shoe is in the box.

7

The shirt is on me.

2

Go and get help!
The cat is up in the tree.

4

Go and get help!
The cat is up in the tree.

1

"I Can Read Story 14"
go – get – help

Get Help!

3

I will get help.

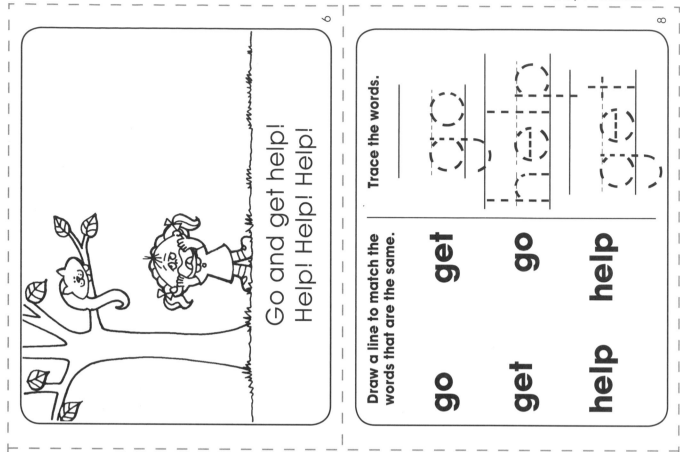

6

Go and get help!
Help! Help! Help!

8

Trace the words.

Draw a line to match the words that are the same.

get	go
go	get
help	help

5

I will get help.

7

Help is here!
The cat is down!

"I Can Read Story 15"
where – are – my

Where Are My Pets?

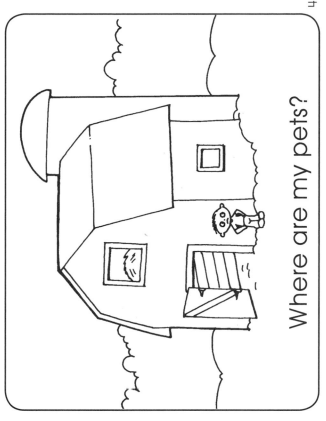

Where are my pets?

Where are my pets?

Are my pets in the barn?

6

Where are my pets?

8

Trace the words.

are

where

my

Draw a line to match the words that are the same.

where   my

are   where

my   are

5

Are my pets in the house?

7

Where are my pets?

2

Where is little dog?
Where is big cat?

4

Up! Up! Up!
That is funny!

1

"I Can Read Story 16"
Review Story

**Help
Little
Dog
and
Big Cat**

3

Look! Little dog
and big cat like to ride.

6

Help! I want to get down!

8

Finish each sentence with words from the story.

1. **Where is** _____ **?**

2. **Help!** _____ **want** _____ **get** _____ **!**

3. **Will** _____ **come** _____ **?**

4. **Up! Up! Up!** _____ **is** _____ **!**

5. **What did little dog and big cat want?**

_____

5

Help! I want to get down!

7

Will you come here?
Get little dog
and big cat down!

"I Can Read Story 17"
said – did – it – jump

See It Jump!

I said, "Did you see it jump?"

I did!

I said, "Did you see it jump?"

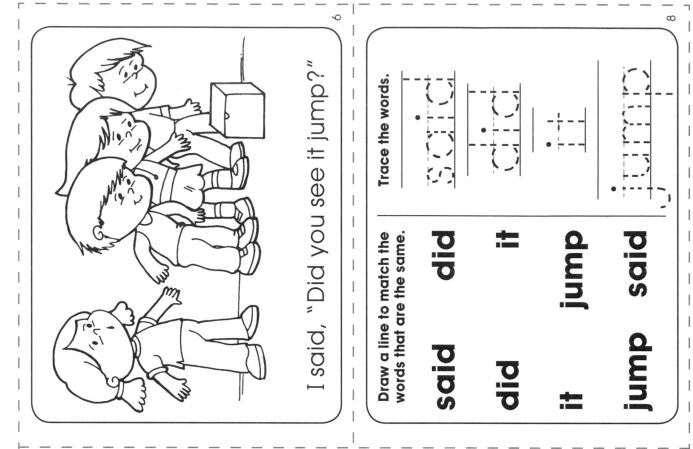

9

I said, "Did you see it jump?"

8

Trace the words.

said

did

it

jump

Draw a line to match the words that are the same.

said   did

it   jump

jump   said

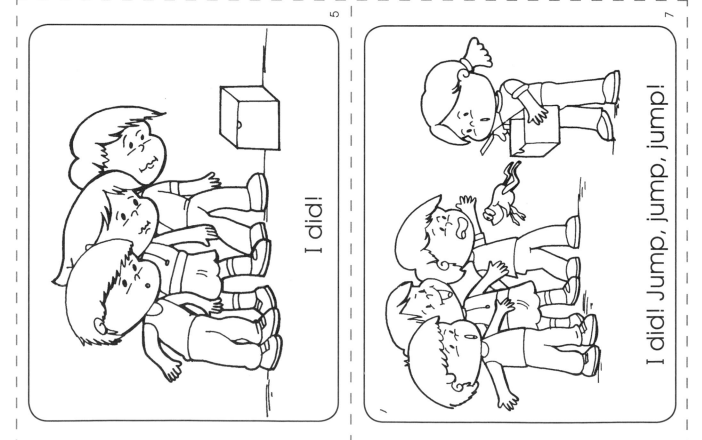

5

I did!

7

I did! Jump, jump, jump!

Who was she?

2

Who was she?

4

"I Can Read Story 18"
who – was – she

Who Was She?

1

She was a big cat.

3

6

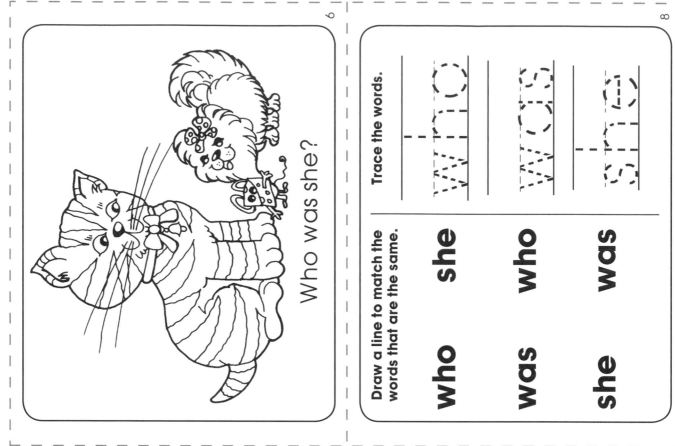

Who was she?

8

Trace the words.

who

was

she

Draw a line to match the words that are the same.

who   she

was   who

she   was

5

She was a little dog.

7

She was a mouse!

2

Where did he go?

4

Where did he go?

"I Can Read Story 19"
he – ran – away

He Ran Away!

1

He ran away.

3

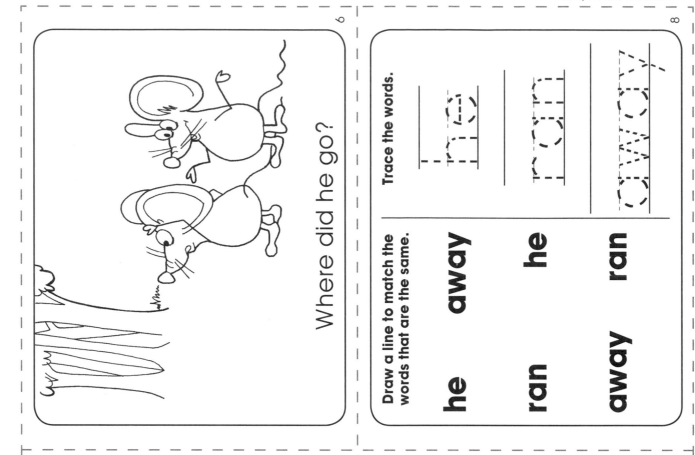

Where did he go?

6

Trace the words.

he

ran

away

Draw a line to match the words that are the same.

he   away

ran   he

away   ran

8

He ran away.

5

He ran and ran and ran!

7

2

Happy Birthday!
This is for you.

4

Happy Birthday!
This is for you.

1

"I Can Read Story 20"
this – for – happy

Happy Birthday!

3

Happy Birthday!
This is for you.

6

Happy Birthday!
This is for you.

8

Trace the words.

for

this

happy

Draw a line to match the words that are the same.

this   for

for   happy

happy   this

5

Happy Birthday!
This is for you.

7

I am happy!
This is my birthday.

I have a
new truck.

2

I have new blocks.

4

"I Can Read Story 21"
have – a – new

New Toys!

TOYS

1

I have a
new doll.

3

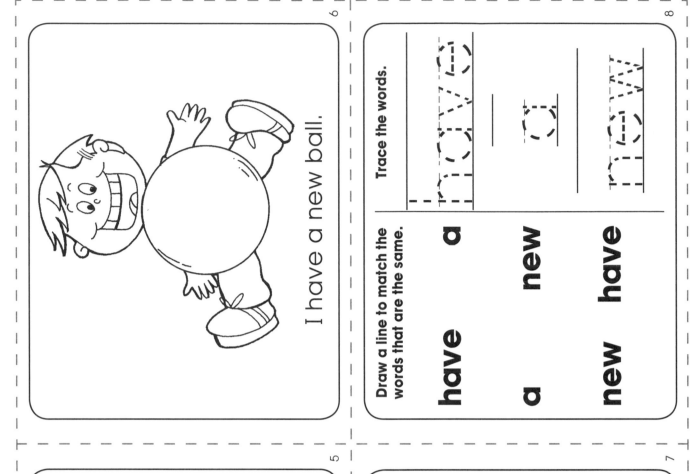

6

I have a new ball.

8

Trace the words.

Draw a line to match the words that are the same.

have   a

a   new

new   have

5

I have
new crayons.

7

We are happy.
We have new toys.

2

Come out and play.

4

Come out and play.

1

"I Can Read Story 22"
no – now – not – out

Come Out
and Play

3

No, not now!

6

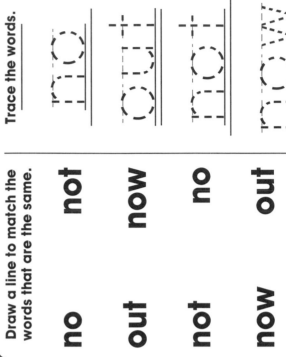

Come out and play.

8

Draw a line to match the words that are the same.

no	out
not	now
now	not
no	now
out	

Trace the words.

no
not
no
now

5

No, not now!

7

Now I can come out and play.

What did you make?

Now what did you make?

"I Can Read Story 23"
make – made – pretty

What Did You Make?

I made pretty playdough.

6

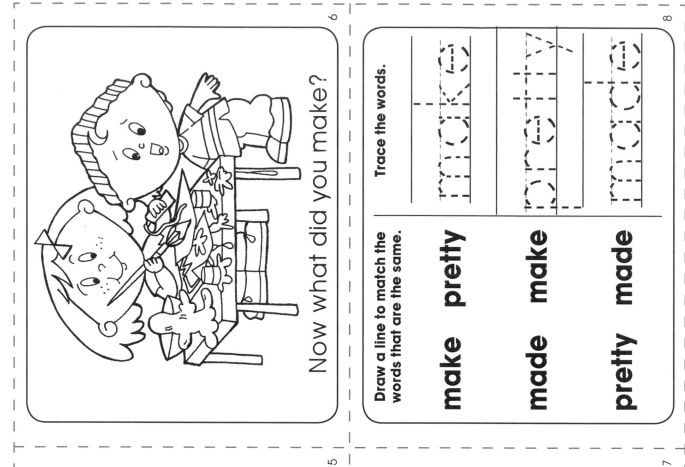

Now what did you make?

8

Trace the words.

make

pretty

make

Draw a line to match the words that are the same.

make   pretty

made   make

pretty   made

5

I made a pretty painting.

7

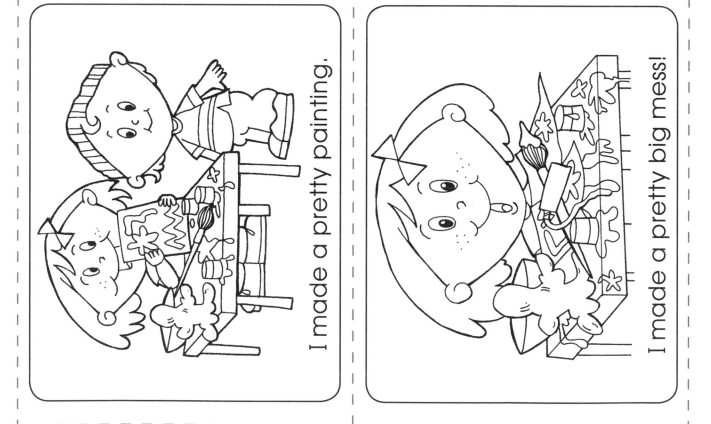

I made a pretty big mess!

2

Who can zip?

4

Who can tie?

1

"I Can Read Story 24"
they – all

Who Can?

3

They all can zip.

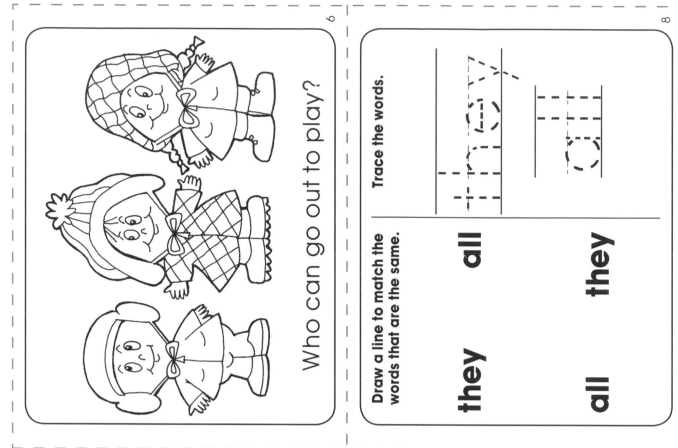

6

Who can go out to play?

5

They all can tie!

8

Trace the words.

Draw a line to match the words that are the same.

they   all

all   they

7

They all can!

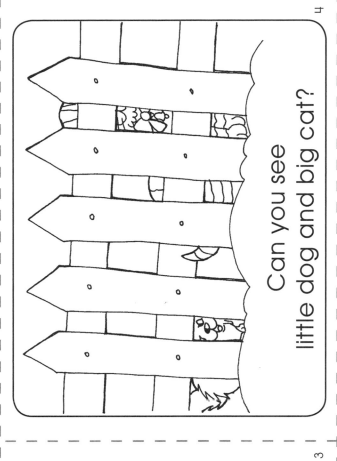

What now, little dog?
What now, big cat?
What did you do?

2

Can you see
little dog and big cat?

4

"I Can Read Story 25"
Review Story

What Did You Do?

1

Where did they go?
What will they do?

3

6

I see you. Do not run away!

8

Draw little dog.

Draw big cat.

5

Come out! One, two, three!
I will find you!

7

You do not look pretty!
You two look funny!

am	at	can	do
all	are	big	did
a	and	away	come

for	find	down
go	get	funny
have	happy	good
here	help	he

is	in	I
like	jump	it
made	look	little
my	me	make

not	one	pretty	run
no	on	play	ride
new	now	out	ran

sees	see	said
the	that	she
three	this	they
two	too	to

was	want	up
where	what	we
with	will	who
	you	yes

bears	bear	barn
bird	bike	beds
box	boy	birthday
cat	button	bug

deer	dolls	dog
fish	elephant	eat
friends	fox	forest
girls	giraffe	frog

hop	house	kitten
merry-go-round	mess	mouse
owl	painting	pets
planes	play dough	puppy

racoon	roller coaster	shirt
shoe	sock	squirrel
swings	toy	toys
trains	tree	zip